PASSPORT FOR THE JOURNEY

21 Day Challenge

Embark on an adventure to become Intentional, Relational, and Perpetual in your relationship with God

By

Tonya J. Brown

PASSPORT FOR THE JOURNEY, 21 Day Challenge

Published by Wild Flower Press, Inc.
P.O. Box 2532
Leland, NC 28451
Website: www.wildflowerpress.biz

ISBN-10: 0-9909616-6-4
ISBN-13: 978-0-9909616-6-6

Cover design by Terry Craig
Photo on front cover © 2006 Tonya J. Brown, used by permission

Scripture quotations are taken from the Holy Bible, New Living Translation, copyright 1996, 2004, 2007 by Tyndale House Foundation. Used by permission of Tyndale House Publishers, Inc., Carol Stream, Illinois 60188. All rights reserved.

DEDICATION

In loving memory of my father,
whose desire to travel lives on in me.
To my husband, daughter and son,
with whom I have traveled many miles.

Itinerary: a plan for a journey

We are all going somewhere. Every day we are faced with choices which define our journey. If we are all going somewhere, shouldn't we have a plan for where we want to go?

I invite you to join me for the next twenty-one days on a journey that is intentional, relational, and perpetual in nature. At times you will find the terrain to be challenging, but the vistas will be worth the effort. You will be urged to respond and encouraged to be on the lookout for how God is already at work around you, and how He desires to work in and through you. He has an itinerary for your journey and offers to reveal it to you.

So grab your passport and be willing to go where He leads. The more you invest the more you will receive.

Bon Voyage!

DEPARTURE

MM. DD YYYY

Intentional: done with purpose

God has a plan for you. He created you with a specific purpose—for this world, in this time. He wants your life to matter.

The first seven days of the trip explore His intentions for your life. The plan is individualized, but you never travel alone. He knows you. He knows the plan. He knows the final destination. He promises to accompany you.

The Bible serves as your map, and the Spirit as your guide. It's time to get started.

*B*efore you were born I set you apart and appointed you as my spokesman to the world. "O Sovereign LORD," I said, "I can't speak for you! I'm too young!" Don't say that, the LORD replied, for you must go wherever I send you and say whatever I tell you. And don't be afraid of the people, for I will be with you and will take care of you. I, the LORD, have spoken!—Jeremiah 1:5-8

We live in a world where instantaneous is our timing preference. We have instant messenger, express mail, and expedia.com. Instant pudding and mashed potatoes sit on our pantry shelves. Yet, when God presents a request, our response is often delayed or accompanied with excuses. God wants a rapid response and His requests come with an unconditional guarantee.

God knew who He was creating before your parents ever knew your gender, eye color, or personality. He set you apart and made some appointments for you. Why not ask Him what He has planned for you today? When He answers, how will you respond? With instantaneous obedience or endless excuses? Don't forget, He promises to protect.

This is what I did.

This is what God did . . .

"**For** I know the plans I have for you," says the Lord. "They are plans for good and not for disaster, to give you a future and a hope."—Jeremiah 29:11

In describing a plan Wikipedia says, "It is commonly understood as a temporal set of intended actions through which one expects to achieve a goal."[i] If we build a house or remodel a room, we have a floor plan. Starting a new business? Better have a business plan. Retail displays use plan-o-grams. Notice that God has multiple plans for us.

God has plans for you and you can be sure that they are good. Do you know what the plan is? Have you asked Him? Too many times we have every line of our To-Do lists and daily planners filled. Have you left room in your plan for *His* plans?

This is what I did . . .

This is what God did . . .

For we are God's masterpiece. He has created us anew in Christ Jesus, so that we can do the good things he planned for us long ago.—Ephesians 2:10

God's story from Genesis to Revelation has been and always will be to restore His created to a relationship with Him. He gave us life. He offers us life after death. But the plan also includes what we are to do with this life: He wants to illustrate His grace in us as an example to others. Now that's a masterpiece!

What crafty good thing does God want to start in you today? Remember you are saved by grace so that you can do good things. In God's amazing story, He takes your life and uses you as an example of His mercy. Ask God which aspect of your life He wants you to surrender to Him so that He can create a new masterpiece. Might it be an attitude, habit, words, or relationship?

This is what I did . . .

This is what God did . . .

Since God chose you to be the holy people he loves, you must clothe yourselves with tenderhearted mercy, kindness, humility, gentleness, and patience. You must make allowance for each other's faults, and forgive the person who offends you. Remember, the Lord forgave you, so you must forgive others.—Colossians 3:12-13

Allowances. We wanted them as kids, the United Kingdom gives them for income tax purposes, and God's Word says that we are to make them for each other's faults. People aren't perfect and we need to accept that and accept them. Instead of stripping others of their dignity, we need to clothe ourselves appropriately.

What articles of clothing do you need to put on today? Do you have on your tenderhearted mercy? Should you accessorize with some gentleness and patience? Are you wearing a good pair of kindness and humility? Don't forget your overcoat of love. If you need a new wardrobe, wisely ask God for one.

This is what I did . . .

This is what God did . . .

When he came to the village of Nazareth . . . he went as usual to the synagogue on the Sabbath and stood up to read the Scriptures. . . . "The Spirit of the LORD is upon me, for he has appointed me to preach Good News to the poor. He has sent me to proclaim that captives will be released, that the blind will see, that the downtrodden will be freed from their oppressors, and that the LORD's favor has come."—Luke 4:16-21

Jesus was in His hometown doing His ordinary thing. In addition to the *where* and *what*, notice *who*. His ministry was to the poor, blind, oppressed and captive. If we are to be like Jesus, then we too must listen to the Spirit and do what He tells us to do.

Who do you know in your town who could use a little Good News? Someone who needs some freedom? A soul who needs your eyes to help them see through their current circumstance? Listen for the Spirit to speak of one who could use some of His favor.

This is what I did . . .

This is what God did . . .

esus replied, "I have already told you, and you don't believe me. The proof is what I do in the name of my Father. But you don't believe me because you are not part of my flock. My sheep recognize my voice; I know them, and they follow me."
—John 10:25-27

A cowboy wrangles his cattle, but a shepherd leads his sheep. Jesus calls us His sheep. Why? Maybe because, like sheep, we tend to congregate together, follow a leader, and are extremely food-oriented. Sheep aren't known for their intelligence, but they are known to recognize and follow the voice of their shepherd.

What Jesus did in His Father's name was proof that He was the Messiah. What you do is proof that you belong to Him. When you listen to, recognize, and obey His voice, others will see you as His. Are you responding to the Good Shepherd's voice? What is He saying to you today?

This is what I did . . .

This is what God did . . .

The LORD gave this message to Jonah son of Amittai: "Get up and go to the great city of Nineveh . . . But Jonah got up and went in the opposite direction . . . "
—Jonah 1:1-3

Then the LORD spoke to Jonah a second time: "Get up and go to the great city of Nineveh, and deliver the message I have given you." This time Jonah obeyed.
—Jonah 3:1-3

Our God is a God of second chances! Someone needs to read that again. Our God is a God of second chances! Not only does He extend us the privilege of becoming involved with His work, He gives us a second chance if we chose to go the opposite direction the first time.

Do you need God to extend a second invitation? Is there a direction He has given you, but you went the opposite way? If so, don't wait for the whale, ask Him to speak it again and this time obey. If you have been following directions in the past, listen for Him to speak a new message. Then get up and go.

This is what I did . . .

This is what God did . . .

Intentional

We are all travelers, but our travels are as varied as individuals are different. However, the travels are for a single purpose, from a single God, who has a single story to tell. The fact that He invites us into His story is amazing.

He invites us to join in the work that He is already doing. Our level of participation is determined by our willingness to get involved. The more willing we are, the more He will entrust us to do. No assignment is too small. It is in the small assignments that trust is built. We learn to trust Him and He in turn entrusts us with more.

How involved did you get in the previous week? Did you listen for His answers? Did you accept the daily challenges?

```
┌─────────────────────────────┐
│  ENTRY                       │
│  ┌───────────────────┐       │
│  │ WEEK 2            │       │
│  └───────────────────┘       │
│  PERMIT                      │
└─────────────────────────────┘
```

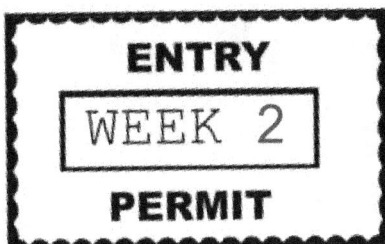

Relational: of or arising from kinship

Unlike a travel agent who sets the itinerary and sets you on your way, God invests His Holy Spirit in you and promises to never leave or forsake you. The Holy Spirit serves as a kind of internal GPS system; but just like that Garmin,[ii] if you don't tune into it, its voice is silenced and you miss your directions.

As the Master storyteller, the omnipotent God, the Author of salvation, and the Guide on the journey invites you not only into His story, but offers to accompany you on your trip. God is relational.

The next week of your travel explores God's desire for relationship with you and His desire for you to be in relationship with others. Better pack some grace and mercy for this trip.

Devote yourselves to prayer with an alert mind and a thankful heart. . . . Pray that I will proclaim this message as clearly as I should. . . . Let your conversation be gracious and effective so that you will have the right answer for everyone.—Colossians 4:2-6

Communication skills are taught through the school system, in the business boardrooms, and on the counselor's couch. It is an essential skill in any relationship. We usually remember our speaking role, but often forget the essential skill of listening. Communication with God is given a special name—prayer. Scripture doesn't merely suggest we pray, it tells us to devote ourselves to communicating with God.

Who are you currently praying for? Are you praying for others? Are you praying for your church's leadership and your country's officials? Do you pray for those who are not believers? Ask God to give you some opportunities to be gracious and effective in your conversations. And don't forget to be alert and thankful for His answers.

This is what I did . . .

This is what God did . . .

" *A* Jewish man was traveling on a trip from Jerusalem to Jericho, and he was attacked by bandits. . . . By chance a Jewish priest came along. . . . A Temple assistant walked over. . . . Then a despised Samaritan came along. . . . Now which of these three would you say was a neighbor to the man who was attacked by bandits?" Jesus asked. The man replied, "The one who showed him mercy."—Luke 10:30-37

An interesting fact about Jericho is that it is situated 846 feet below sea level; making it the lowest permanently inhabited site on earth. This man was on his way to Jericho. Ironically, he was coming from the Holy City and traveling to the lowest city. On his way down, he gets beat up and left half dead. Most of us can probably relate on some level. Luckily a neighbor showed him some mercy.

If you have asked God to save you, then you've received some mercy. So now go and do the same. Ask God to show you who is on their way down and needs a dose of tender loving mercy.

This is what I did . . .

This is what God did . . .

i am going to boast only about my weaknesses. I have plenty to boast about and would be no fool in doing it. . . . But to keep me from getting puffed up, I was given a thorn in my flesh. . . .Three different times I begged the LORD to take it away. Each time he said, "My gracious favor is all you need. My power works best in your weakness."
—2 Corinthians 12:5-9

Most of us don't broadcast our failures on billboards; actually, we usually do our best to conceal them in a closet. We may even beg God to take them away. Yet God says that He works most powerfully through our worst failures.

Are you willing to humble yourself before someone else in order for God to do some powerful work? Ask God to show you someone who is currently suffering because of a mistake they made. Share how God's grace was sufficient in your failure. Then watch His power work through your weakness.

This is what I did . . .

This is what God did . . .

TRAVEL PERMIT

DAY 11

> *A*ll this newness of life is from God, who brought us back to himself through what Christ did. And God has given us the task of reconciling people to him. . . . We are Christ's ambassadors and God is using us to speak to you. We urge you, as though Christ himself were here pleading with you, "Be reconciled to God!"
> —2 Corinthians 5:18, 20

Dictionary.com defines *reconcile* as a verb meaning to "restore friendly relations between."[iii]   God wants us to restore some friendly relations between us and Him, us and others, and even us and our past. He views all of these in a friendly way and so should we. Amputate any of these vital relationships and the Body of Christ is incomplete.

How friendly are you with God, others, and your past? What relationship does God desire to help you redeem today? Do you need to spend some time building your relationship with Jesus, dealing with a sinful past, or becoming an ambassador to others for Him?

This is what I did . . .

This is what God did . . .

He is the source of every mercy and the God who comforts us. He comforts us in all our troubles so that we can comfort others.—2 Corinthians 1:3-4a

Deep and serious wounds do not disappear, they leave a scar. They are visible. Others notice these marks and usually react to them by either inquiring about them or being repulsed by them. Owners of the scars can brag about them or be embarrassed by them. Although the reaction is opposite, it is equally powerful. People with past hurts often need to be comforted. People with scars can comfort people with scars.

What in your life has caused the deepest wound? Chances are, even recalling it now has caused pain. Will you let God comfort your hurt? This may have been your first time of feeling His comfort or it may be a wound He has continually comforted. Someone else is suffering from a similar wound. Would you consider revealing your scar in order to offer comfort to another?

This is what I did . . .

This is what God did . . .

God blesses you when you are mocked and persecuted and lied about because you are my followers. Be happy about it! Be very glad! For a great reward awaits you in heaven. And remember, the ancient prophets were persecuted, too.
—Matthew 5:11-12

Don't worry. Be happy. These words may get credited to the Indian mystic Meher Baba or the vocalist Bobby McFerrin, but God gave us that directive in His Holy Word and illustrates it through His ancient prophets. Jesus included this in His "be attitudes." And He didn't stop at "be happy," He challenges us to "be very glad" even in the face of opposition.

What opposition are you up against as you follow Jesus in showing love in a wicked world? If you are feeling some persecution, know that you are in good company. The ancient prophets felt it. The apostles experienced it. Jesus, Himself, was not immune to it. Ask God to heal your wounds and give you the strength to carry on. The reward awaits and is great. Be very glad.

This is what I did . . .

This is what God did . . .

The Kingdom of Heaven can be compared to a king who decided to bring his accounts up to date with servants who had borrowed money from him. In the process, one of his debtors was brought in who owed him millions of dollars. . . .

"Please, be patient with me, and I will pay it all." Then his master was filled with pity for him, and he released him and forgave his debt. But when the man left the king, he went to a fellow servant who owed him a few thousand dollars. He grabbed him by the throat and demanded instant payment.
—Matthew 18:23-24, 26b-30

Go to jail. Go directly to jail. But who is going? Our enemy or us? When we choose to forgive, we not only let the enemy go, we free ourselves from the prison of unforgiveness.

Are you currently holding prisoners? Ask God to search your heart for any unforgiveness. Forgiveness is not a gift to the deserving. Not one deserves it. Not even you. But you received it and God wants you to regift it.

This is what I did . . .

This is what God did . . .

Intentional . . . Relational

Relationships are a challenging part of our journey with God, but a journey worth taking. Jesus made the trip when He came to earth as a baby in a manger, carried a cross up Calvary, submitted to the mob and the tomb, defeated death, and ascended to heaven.

Jesus knows about being relational and was willing to die in order to restore your relationship with the Father. He was willing to live and model godly relationships with boundaries during His time on earth.

God is all about unity. Therefore, Satan is all about division. With godliness as your goal, and with the Holy Spirit as your guide, when you choose to be relational, you choose to be like your God.

Perpetual: continuing without interruption; ceaseless.

Trips are motivated by a variety of intentions. Some trips are intended for business and some for pleasure. Some are to celebrate an occasion or to mourn a loss. Trips can be taken via different modes of transportation. You can fly the friendly skies, take a trip by train, or caravan by car.

No matter the motive or the mode, most trips must come to an end. Your itinerary has departure and arrival dates set in advance. Sometimes you are happy to return home, but other times the trip is so enticing that the end comes too soon.

Not so with this journey. Once you embark, you never have to stop. During the remainder of your time on earth you are merely a sojourner on your way to a heavenly home. God uses this time to accomplish His purposes on this earth and to prepare you for that home. Your journey with God is not only intentional and relational, it is also perpetual.

> **The** Kingdom of Heaven is like a mustard seed planted in a field. It is the smallest of all seeds, but it becomes the largest of garden plants . . .
> —Matthew 13:31-32

Small seeds. Big results. That is how Jesus describes His Kingdom. He used a mustard seed to illustrate His point. What might He use to convey that point to His people today in the US? Maybe kudzu? Anyone who travels much in the Southeast knows kudzu by sight if not by name. It's that plant that covers all the trees. Not the Spanish moss of Savannah, but the vines outside of Dahlonega. Its seed is the size of a pea, but soon the plant takes over. It not only covers the trees, but also houses, cars, or anything else that sits still.

Ask God what small deed you could do today that He could use for big results in His kingdom. Our God is big enough to use your kind word, friendly gesture, helping hand, or encouraging smile to impact eternity. Infest your community with a covering of kindness.

This is what I did . . .

This is what God did . . .

The Kingdom of Heaven is like the yeast a woman used in making bread. Even though she put only a little yeast in three measures of flour, it permeated every part of the dough.—Matthew 13:33

In case we didn't get it the first time, Jesus follows up on His first story with a second and similar story. On the heels of the mustard seed tale, He tells one about yeast. From the garden to the kitchen the theme remains the same. Small ingredient. Big impact. Bakers would understand that making yeast pastry takes more work, but the results can be boiled down to the difference between a cracker and a Krispy Kreme.

God is the Ancient of Days, but He doesn't have Alzheimer's. He didn't tell the yeast parable because He forgot that He had already told the mustard seed one. He told it because it matters and He didn't want us to forget. What small good does God want you to do today that He can cook into something sweet? Go ahead and ask Him. He has an answer for you.

This is what I did . . .

This is what God did . . .

Yes, I am the vine; you are the branches. Those who remain in me, and I in them, will produce much fruit. For apart from me you can do nothing. Anyone who does not remain in me is thrown away like a useless branch and withers. . . . My true disciples produce much fruit. This brings great glory to my Father.—John 15:5-8

Gardening is hard work. It is done under the sun and in the heat. It burns our skin and blisters our fingers. But notice that we are not the ones doing the work. God is the gardener. He's doing the pruning. Jesus is the vine. He's doing the growing. Our role is to just be the branches.

Jesus loves you and He wants you to love others. What does the Gardener want to prune out of your life so that you can produce a bumper crop of love and joy? It may sound painful, but stick around for the pruning. The harvest is glorious.

This is what I did . . .

This is what God did . . .

Remember this—a farmer who plants only a few seeds will get a small crop. But the one who plants generously will get a generous crop. You must each make up your own mind as to how much you should give. Don't give reluctantly or in response to pressure. For God loves a person who gives cheerfully.—2 Corinthians 9:6-7

The stock market has looked more like a roller coaster in the past few years than a ladder. Terms like recession and depression are a dime a dozen in the news. But one investment that guarantees a steady growth is the commodity of love. God has generously given love to us and expects us to lavishly unleash it on others—not because we have to, but because we want to.

What kind of exchange rate does love have in your life? Are you receiving and investing or securing and stockpiling? If you take and advance the abundant love that God has given to you, your life will be rich. You can take that to the bank.

This is what I did . . .

This is what God did . . .

*B*ut if anyone has enough money to live well and sees a brother or sister in need and refuses to help—how can God's love be in that person? Dear children, let us stop just saying we love each other; let us show it by our actions.—1 John 3:17-18

Our world seems to be obsessed with extremes. We had a reality television Extreme Makeover show that expanded to Home Edition and Weight Loss Edition. Even the P90 home fitness program went extreme. Yet there is nothing new about being extreme. Jesus was the extreme savior. He didn't just give a new look, He gave His life so that we can live a forgiven life here and an eternal life in the hereafter.

The Bible says you should be willing to give like Jesus gave. He saw your circumstances, saw a need—then filled it. By going to extremes to help someone else in need, you are showing them how much both you and God love them. Are you willing to let others see God's love through you? Get extreme.

Does your life or just your song worship Christ? Keep your conscience clear so that others can plainly see you practicing a triple threat combination of hope, faith, and love. Is that humanly possible? No, but let Christ be LORD of your life and nothing is impossible.

This is what I did . . .

This is what God did . . .

Instead, you must worship Christ as Lord of your life. And if you are asked about your Christian hope, always be ready to explain it. But you must do this in a gentle and respectful way. Keep your conscious clear. Then if people speak evil against you, they will be ashamed when they see what a good life you live because you belong to Christ.—1 Peter 3:15-16

Our lives are on display for others to see. What they should see exhibited are hope and faith and love—displayed in a gentle and respectful way. What a combination and, oh, the possibilities of such a life! A life like that should draw some attention and inquiring minds should want to know where these qualities come from. Be ready to give an answer . . . it's because we belong to Christ.

This is what I did . . .

This is what God did . . .

Those who live only to satisfy their own sinful desires will harvest the consequences of decay and death. But those who live to please the Spirit will harvest everlasting life from the Spirit. So don't get tired of doing what is good. Don't get discouraged and give up.
—Galatians 6:8-9

Let's face it. Churches have a reputation for putting on a show and sealing it with an Amen on their way out. A grand entrance with a grand exit. We have revivals, VBS, and church camps that each last about a week. A sermon series spans a few weeks. Bible studies usually buckle down for seven to twelve weeks. These are all great, but God made us to live for eternity and everlasting.

How will you live? Will you live to satisfy self or the Spirit? This decision will have everlasting results. The good that you do today, tomorrow, next week, and in the years to come will bless you. So be encouraged. You may get tired, but keep the faith and don't give up.

This is what I did . . .

This is what God did . . .

Intentional, Relational, Perpetual

Twenty-one days of training for the rest of your days.

Be intentional about where you are going, the choices you are making, the relationships you are building, and the good that you are doing. You didn't make this trip to merely gather souvenirs; you made it to equip yourself for the rest of the journey with your Sovereign.

Retrace your steps to remind yourself of the plan, but never rest on your laurels. Each new day is an opportunity to fulfill what God has planned for you to do this day. Tune in to Him, follow Him, and share Him with all you meet along the way.

Bon Voyage!

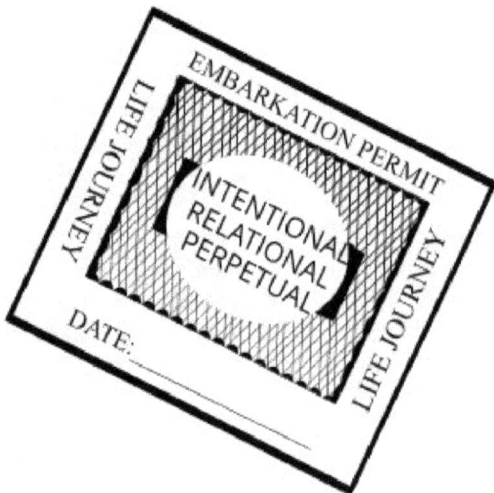

ENDNOTES

i   Page 8, "plan": https://en.wikipedia.org/wiki/Plan, (May 25, 2015)

ii   Page 21 Garmin: A a widely-known name for a variety of GPS guidance devices for automotive, aviation, marine, outdoor, and sports uses

iii   Page 28 "reconcile":
http://www.dictionary.com/browse/reconcile
(accessed: March 25, 2015)

Thank you for purchasing and reading this book!

If you enjoyed it, please take a moment to review it online through your retailer's website or the
Wild Flower Press, Inc. Facebook page!

About the Author

Tonya Brown is a traveler who makes mistakes during her journey. However, she has learned that even when she is unfaithful to God, He is always faithful to her. She has experienced the grace and love of her Savior and desires to share this good news with her fellow sojourners. Her writings challenge the reader to consider and make intentional choices along the journey in order to reach the desired destination.

Tonya is a wife, mother, grandmother, teacher, and mentor coach with a passion for teaching God's Word and establishing mentoring relationships with women experiencing difficult circumstances. Her hobbies include hiking in the mountains and strolling on the beach. She enjoys seeing new places and learning new things.

Other Books by this Publisher

What Mama Never Told You about the Afterlife by Terry L. Craig is an apologetic written in simple language to address "Christian Universalism"—the idea that all people are saved regardless of their beliefs.

Like fiction with a message?

Stephanie Bennett—*Within the Walls* trilogy:
Within the Walls, Breaking the Silence, and *The Poet's Treasure* (Futuristic Fiction)

Terry L. Craig—*Fellowship of the Mystery* trilogy:
Gatekeeper, Sojourner, and *Swordsman* (Apocalyptic Science Fiction)

Terry L. Craig—NEW SERIES ("Steampunk" Scifi):
Scions of the Aegean C. Book 1, *Descent into the Wild*s is now available, Book 2, *Through the Land of Cloud and Leaf* launching in 2016

All of our books are available as paperbacks or ebooks at Amazon.com, CreateSpace, Smashwords, and many other fine book retailers.

To purchase paperback copies of any of our books or to read some of our free articles and studies, visit Wild Flower Press, Inc. on the web at:

www.wildflowerpress.biz

www.ingramcontent.com/pod-product-compliance
Lightning Source LLC
Chambersburg PA
CBHW071934020426
42331CB00010B/2861